THE
RED CROSS
AND THE
RED CRESCENT

First New Discovery Books Edition 1994

Originally published in Great Britain in 1992
by Exley Publications Ltd, 16 Chalk Hill, Watford,
Herts WD1 4BN, United Kingdom.

Copyright © 1992 Exley Publications
Copyright © 1992 Michael Pollard

New Discovery Books
Macmillan Publishing Company
866 Third Avenue
New York, NY 10022

Macmillan Publishing Company is part of the
Maxwell Communication Group of Companies.

First Edition
10 9 8 7 6 5 4 3 2 1

Series editor: Helen Exley

Printed and bound by Gráficas Reunidas S.A., Madrid, Spain.

Picture Credits: AKG: 10/11, 26 (bottom), 37 (top), 47 (both), 48; Gamma: 4 (bottom), 5, 6 (bottom), 16
(bottom), 23 (bottom), 52, 53 (bottom right); Hulton/Keystone: 34; Image Select: 35; International Committee of
the Red Cross and Red Crescent: 8, 9, 11 (top), 12 (top), 13 (top), 14 (middle), 15, 16 (top), 18, (middle), 19
(middle), 21, 23 (top), 24 (both), 25 (top), 33, 36, 39 (top), 41, 42 (all), 44, 46, 50, 53 (top left and right), 54 (all),
56 (both), 57 (both), 59, 60; League of Red Cross and Red Crescent Societies: 4 (top), 6 (top), 7, 16 (middle), 18
(top left and right), 19 (top left and right and bottom right); Mansell Collection: 20, 26 (top); Mary Evans: 25
(bottom), 28 (both), 30 (both), 32, 45; Red Cross: cover, 14 (top and margin), 17, 43; Roger Viollet: 13 (bottom),
22, 29, 31, 39 (bottom); Sipa Press: 51: United Nations High Commissioner for Refugees: 37 (bottom).

Library of Congress Cataloging-in-Publication Data
Pollard, Michael, 1931-
⠀⠀⠀The Red Cross and the Red Crescent / Michael Pollard.
⠀⠀⠀⠀⠀p.⠀⠀cm. — (Organizations that help the world)
⠀⠀⠀Includes bibliographical references and index.
⠀⠀⠀ISBN 0-02-774720-4
⠀⠀⠀⠀⠀1. League of Red Cross and Red Crescent Societies — History
⠀— Juvenile literature. [1. Red Cross — History. 2. League of
Red Cross and Red Crescent Societies — History.] I. Title. II.
Series.
HV568.P65 1994
⠀⠀⠀361.7'634'09 — dc20⠀⠀⠀⠀⠀⠀⠀⠀⠀⠀⠀⠀⠀⠀⠀⠀93-26383
Summary: Provides an in-depth look at the several branches of the
Red Cross, from its inception to the present.

■ ORGANIZATIONS ■
THAT HELP THE WORLD

THE
RED CROSS
AND THE
RED CRESCENT

by MICHAEL POLLARD

new
Discovery
B·O·O·K·S
New York

*Above: June 1990.
Rescuers search the ruins
of the town of Rudbar,
Iran, looking, listening,
and hoping for signs of
life. This is delicate work.
Any careless move might
make the wreckage settle
and cause further
casualties.
Right: Working with bare
hands and shovels,
rescuers desperately clear
through the rubble at
Manjil, while a survivor
waits for news.*

Earthquake!

Iran, June 21, 1990. As night fell peacefully over the mountains northwest of the capital, Tehran, there was no hint of the terror to come. By half-past midnight most families in the towns and villages were asleep.

Then, at thirty-one minutes after midnight, disaster struck. Without warning, a major earthquake brought death and destruction to the mountain communities. The initial quake was followed by aftershocks. When these had subsided, nearly forty thousand people were dead, another sixty thousand were injured, and about half a million were made homeless. Many thousands more were trapped in the ruins of their homes, awaiting the arrival of rescue teams. Panic-stricken survivors fought their way out of the shattered homes into the streets, where they gathered, dazed and terrified. Some went back to their homes to rescue pets or to collect treasured possessions — only to be caught and trapped by the aftershocks.

The Red Crescent Society mobilized ten thousand staff and volunteers to help after the earthquake in Iran in 1990. For ten days and ten nights rescue workers from all over the world searched the remains of the mountain communities. Here, a French worker uses a specially trained dog to detect any sign of life in the ruined town of Manjil.

In 1984 and 1985, drought
hit the Sahel region of
Africa. Crops failed and
the people starved.
Television pictures alerted
the world and a massive
food relief operation began.
Above: Grain is distributed
from a Red Cross store.
Right: The Red Cross and
Red Crescent Movement
throws huge resources into
major relief efforts. Here,
the ICRC's own aircraft
bring food to starving
children staying in a relief
camp, where they are being
restored to health.

The quake had brought down telephone lines, cut electricity supplies, and blocked roads, so it was some hours before news of the disaster reached Tehran and, through Tehran, the outside world. But as soon as the extent of the damage and injuries was known, a network of national and international aid swung into action.

First on the scene were the trained rescue teams of the Red Crescent Society of the Islamic Republic of Iran, flown in by helicopter because the roads were impassable. Iran has a long history of earthquakes, and one of the main activities of its Red Crescent Society is to train volunteers in disaster preparedness and rescue techniques. But no amount of training could prepare the teams for what they were to find in the mountains on that June morning. One of the first leaders to arrive described the scene like this: "Townspeople were clawing at the rubble with their bare hands, calling out to us to help them. Many were in shock and wanted to pull us to their homes.

"We were administering first aid and a lot of painkillers and selecting those who would not live if they did not fly out immediately. We could not think of the dead. We could do nothing for them and we could not spend time digging. We had to give priority to the living."

The world helps

Within a few days, the Red Crescent Society had mobilized a force of ten thousand staff and volunteers. They combed the ruins for survivors, carried the injured to hospitals, drove trucks bringing in food, blankets, tents, and medical supplies, and set up feeding points for the homeless. By this time, relief for the Iranian earthquake disaster had become an international operation. Reacting as it always does to human suffering anywhere in the world, the International Red Cross and Red Crescent Movement mounted an operation that brought supplies from overseas ranging from cooking equipment to medicines and special aids for the injured.

It was ten days before the rescue teams, working

The Red Crescent Society of the Islamic Republic of Iran was itself a victim of the 1990 earthquake when the shock undermined this office building. All the roads were impassable, so helicopters were used to transport rescue workers to those areas most affected.

In 1989, the International Federation of Red Cross and Red Crescent National Societies launched thirty-nine international appeals for two and a half million victims in thirty-three countries. Nineteen of these appeals were in response to natural disasters such as floods and hurricanes.

all day and all night from one ruined building to the next, could announce that all the survivors had been brought out and taken into care. The immediate emergency had passed, but there was now the long process of rebuilding the homes and lives of the people of the mountain communities.

Here again, international help was directed through the International Federation of Red Cross and Red Crescent Societies to back up the efforts of Iran's own Red Crescent Society. Among the most urgently needed items were water purification systems, portable generators to provide power for the temporary camps and emergency hospitals, and medical equipment, such as kidney machines and blood transfusion kits. Warm, weatherproof housing would be needed to see the surviving families through the cold mountain winter. People all over the world responded to the plight of the Iranians and gave practical help through the national appeals launched by the Red Cross and Red Crescent.

The Iranian earthquake was only one of more than twenty natural disasters worldwide in 1990 that called on the resources of the Red Cross and Red Crescent Movement. In the same year, the movement organized aid for the victims of war and civil war in three continents. Altogether, 1990 saw the launch of no fewer than forty international appeals aimed at helping four and a half million victims of natural and man-made disasters.

Meanwhile, far away from the places that were attracting the headlines, the everyday work of the movement, involving one hundred million members and volunteer workers throughout the world, went on. This work has one single aim: the relief of human suffering wherever it occurs.

An international network

The International Red Cross and Red Crescent Movement is the largest organization in the world devoted to the care of people in all kinds of circumstances where they may need help. Where there is human suffering, the movement does not recognize boundaries, different races, or differences in religious beliefs. In a world of calamities brought about by hostile environments and the inhumane actions of peoples to each other, the work of the International Red Cross and Red Crescent Movement is a cause for hope. It is a practical expression of the belief that we all share one world and that what happens to any of us is the responsibility of all.

How it began

The International Red Cross and Red Crescent Movement's efforts to save humankind from suffering and distress began in the most unlikely place — on a battlefield. The story started over one hundred and thirty years ago.

In the summer of 1859, French and Austrian troops fought a battle near the village of Solferino in northern Italy. War is never anything other than cruel, but in those days battles were fought with unrelieved savagery. Soldiers often killed any prisoners they took to steal their belongings. The wounded often had either to look after themselves or were left to rot and die. There were few doctors or nurses to attend them, and there was nowhere to move them for treatment.

As for the survivors, they had to find their own way home, and anyone trying to help them was likely to be attacked. The dead were often left unburied and there was no way of letting their families know what had happened. Once soldiers had fought their battles, whether they had survived or died, been wounded or taken prisoner, they were forgotten

Troops went into the Battle of Solferino almost drugged with the excitement of war. "It seemed," said one French soldier, "as if the wind was carrying us forward. The smell of powder, the noise of the guns, drums beating and bugles sounding, it all puts life into you and stirs you up!" But for many, this mood was short-lived. Thirty thousand men, as Jean-Henri Dunant reported, ended the day "lying helpless on the naked ground in their own blood."

by their commanders and often by their comrades.

The Battle of Solferino raged for the sixteen hours of daylight one long June day. By the time it was over, with the Austrian army in retreat, thirty thousand men — one in ten of those taking part — were dead and another ten thousand were wounded. The suffering of the wounded and the battle-shocked survivors was terrible. Food was in short supply and drinking water was polluted. There were no dressings or bandages. Disease soon began to spread, not only among the soldiers, but also among the people of the Solferino district.

An observer at the front

Yet this was how battles had been fought for thousands of years. But at Solferino there was an observer of the aftermath of the battle who had never seen the results of war at firsthand before, and who was horrified to find out how much suffering is involved. He was Jean-Henri Dunant, a thirty-year-old Swiss citizen who, on a business trip to meet with Emperor Napoleon III, had arrived accidentally at the end of the battle.

Below: Napoleon III surveys the battlefield of Solferino — from a safe distance. The French and their allies had at their disposal 150,000 men and 400 artillery pieces. Facing them were 170,000 Austrian troops with 500 heavy guns.

Many other people of Dunant's age and background would merely have turned away in despair, but Dunant forced himself to walk among the dead. "Bodies of men and horses covered the battlefield," he remembered later. "Corpses were strewn over roads, ditches, ravines, thickets and fields; the approaches of Solferino were literally thick with dead.... Some of the soldiers who lay dead had a calm expression, those who had been killed outright. But many were disfigured by the torments of the death-struggle, their limbs stiffened, their bodies blotched with ghastly spots, their hands clawing at the ground, their eyes staring wildly...."

But it was the suffering of the wounded that affected Dunant most: "With faces black with the flies that swarmed about their wounds, men gazed around them, wild-eyed and helpless.... There was one poor man, completely disfigured, with a broken jaw and his swollen tongue hanging out of his mouth. I moistened his dry lips and hardened tongue, took a handful of lint and dipped it in the bucket they were carrying behind me, and squeezed the water from the improvised sponge into the deformed opening that had been his mouth."

Faced with so much suffering, one person could do little, but Dunant set about organizing the women

Jean-Henri Dunant followed Napoleon to Italy to plead for concessions for his business. But the suffering he saw led him to neglect his business affairs and fight for the wounded.

of the nearby town of Castiglione to give the wounded food and drink and to wash and dress their wounds. The town's small boys fetched and carried water and ran other errands. Castiglione's churches were turned into hospitals.

After the battle

When, at last, the dead had been buried and the more seriously wounded were transferred to hospitals in Milan and other cities, Jean-Henri Dunant had time to reflect on what he had seen.

Two things struck him. The first was the sheer ugliness of war: the noise, the destruction, the death, the brutality. He noted how quickly the false hopes of glory that soldiers took into battle vanished when the fighting was over. It seemed exciting to go to war — but the excitement soon deteriorated into horror, bloodshed, and pain. The second impression Dunant gained was of the willingness of volunteers to help *if there was someone to organize them and show them what to do.*

When Jean-Henri Dunant returned to Switzerland, his haunting memories of Solferino went with him. He poured them out three years later in a book, *A Memory of Solferino,* describing what he had seen and putting forward ideas for making the consequences of war less horrifying.

These ideas included training teams of volunteers in each country for medical service in wartime, the planning in advance of food, water, and medical supplies for the wounded, the provision of ambulances, and arrangements to let the families of dead and wounded soldiers know what had happened

Above: An Afghan miniature, used as a poster. In 1863 and 1864, Jean-Henri Dunant became a familiar figure in the world's government offices as he drummed up interest in the forthcoming diplomatic conference which was to sign the first Geneva Convention. His persistence paid off, and sixteen nations went to the conference.

Right: Out of Dunant's horror at the chaos and suffering of the Battle of Solferino came the International Red Cross and Red Crescent Movement. However, Dunant's devotion to the movement cost him dearly: At the age of thirty-nine he was bankrupt and he lost his position in the Red Cross.

to them. The wounded on the battlefield, and people who were looking after them, should be regarded as neutral, whichever side they came from, and therefore safe from attack by either side.

Dunant's ideas caught the attention of four of Geneva's leading citizens who were already involved in charity work for the poor and needy. Early in 1863 these four, with Dunant, formed a "Committee of Five" that they named the International Committee for Relief to the Wounded. It was the beginning of the International Red Cross and Red Crescent Movement.

Across frontiers

From the start, it was clear that if there was to be a plan to help the wounded in battle, the plan must be accepted internationally. There would be no point in having an agreement if only one country taking part in a war had signed it. So the first action of the Committee of Five was to call an international conference to discuss the plan.

This in itself was a new idea. There had been international conferences before, but their purpose had been to divide up countries among the victors in war. No one had ever called nations together to discuss ideas for lessening human suffering.

Above: General Guilluame-Henri Dufour was one of the members of the "Committee of Five" formed in Geneva. Then in his seventies, he had had a distinguished military career, so he was able to speak with authority on the suffering that the Red Cross Movement hoped to alleviate.

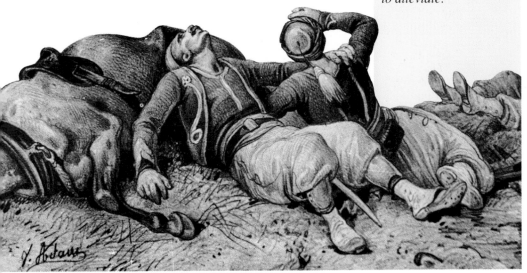

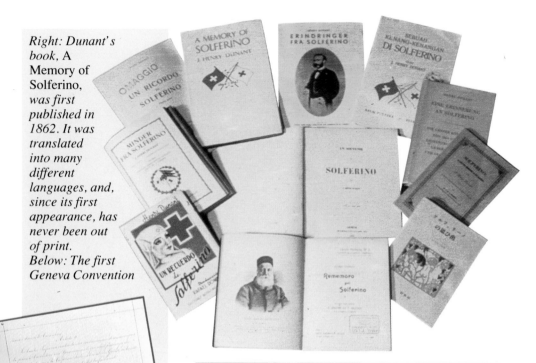

*Right: Dunant's
book,* A
Memory of
Solferino, *was first
published in
1862. It was
translated
into many
different
languages, and,
since its first
appearance, has
never been out
of print.
Below: The first
Geneva Convention*

*Right: The signing
ceremony at Geneva's
town hall. When it was
the British delegate's
turn to sign, he needed
an official seal. General
Dufour cut a button
from the diplomat's
military tunic and said,
"There...you have the
arms of Her Majesty."*

The conference met in Geneva in October
1863, and representatives from sixteen countries
attended. A detailed plan for the treatment of
wounded soldiers was drawn up for the
representatives to take back to their own
governments for discussion. The movement, led by
the Committee of Five, also adopted a red cross on a
white background as its symbol. This was to be used
on war ambulances, military hospitals, and the

uniforms of army medical staff, as well as by volunteers, as a sign that they were neutral and not to be attacked. It now became known as the Red Cross Movement.

The following year, at a second conference in Geneva, twelve countries signed the world's first international agreement on the conduct of war. This agreement was called the first Geneva Convention. It laid down ten rules, or articles, for the treatment of the wounded on the battlefield, based on the plan drawn up the year before. The signatories were all European and all Christian countries. These countries had either already set up societies within their countries, known as National Societies, to train volunteers or were planning to do so. Each National Society organized its services in relation to its country's needs. Later, the twelve were joined by others — but the Red Cross Movement still had to spread beyond Christian Europe.

The doubters

Not everyone welcomed the Geneva Convention. To many people, it seemed strange to suggest that wars should be fought according to rules, as if they were games. Surely, they said, war represented the complete absence of rules, except one: the strongest side won. How could there be laws of war? It would be better, some people argued, to work for the end of all wars. Then the question of how to treat the wounded would not arise.

No one doubted that the end of war would be an admirable aim, but the founders of the Red Cross were realistic enough to see that, although this might be achieved one day, it was a long way off. Meanwhile, the horrors of war would continue, but at least some of the suffering could be relieved.

The peacemakers were not the only people who were uneasy about the Geneva Convention. Many senior army officers had their doubts, too. Some suspected that the Red Cross symbol might be used by spies as a cover to enable them to penetrate enemy lines, or to protect military buildings, such as arms stores, or fake "ambulances" full of troops

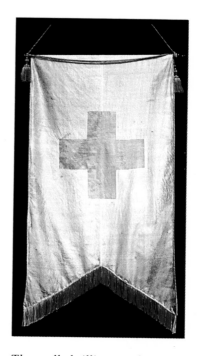

The really brilliant stroke in the creation of the Red Cross was the adoption of a simple emblem that could be stitched together or painted easily, even in the heat of the battlefield: the Swiss flag reversed. This was the very first Red Cross banner — the first appearance of a symbol that was to become universally recognized and respected.

*Right: The International
Committee of the Red
Cross is based in Geneva.
It is responsible for
questions relating to the
Geneva Conventions as
well as spreading
knowledge of humanitarian
law. It supervises the
exchange of prisoners of
war. Here, an ICRC
delegate briefs observers
on the rules of war laid
down by the four Geneva
Conventions.*

*Right: The International
Federation of Red Cross
and Red Crescent Societies
(originally called the
League of Red Cross
Societies) coordinates
health care and relief work.
In a disaster, it acts as an
intermediary between the
affected area and the
world's National Societies
wishing to offer help. Here,
food relief goes through the
International Federation
on its way to China.*

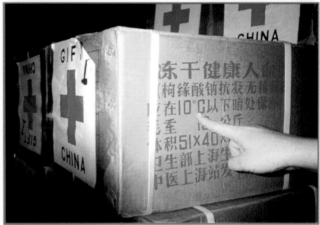

*Right: There are National
Red Cross or Red Crescent
Societies in virtually every
country of the world. They
undertake a variety of
work, including first aid
and disaster training,
health care, disease
prevention, and, in many
countries, the operation of
emergency services. This
team of trained Mexican
Red Cross workers is
giving aid at the scene of
an air crash.*

ready for action. There were also concerns about practical problems in the heat of battle. Wouldn't Red Cross teams get in the way? And would it be possible to avoid firing on them by accident?

There was another objection even from people who approved of the principles of the movement. The Geneva Convention depended on the existence in each country of a National Society to train and organize medical teams for use in wartime. Each National Society needed the approval of its country's government, but it also needed to be able to act independently. There were fears in some countries that, in wartime, the army would take over the societies. In others, leaders of the National Societies wanted to undertake work — such as giving financial help to the families of soldiers — which was outside the movement's original aims. These problems were solved by the International Committee of the Red Cross in Geneva developing rules for the National Societies so that they all had guaranteed independence from their governments and all had the same single aim: medical help for the wounded. Meanwhile, the International Committee of the Red Cross itself undertook the work of persuading countries to sign the Geneva Convention and of checking that its articles were observed in wartime.

Organization

This division in activities continues today. From Geneva, the International Committee of the Red Cross oversees the observance of the four Geneva Conventions and the "Additional Protocols" that have also been added. The International Federation of Red Cross and Red Crescent Societies, also in Geneva, coordinates international relief efforts in major peacetime disasters, like the Iranian earthquake of 1990. The National Societies operate in almost every country in the world, working within their own boundaries. These National Red Cross or Red Crescent Societies train young people and adult volunteers in first aid, rescue work, and disaster survival. In some countries such as

"We were not dreaming when we expressed the hope that men, not enrolled in the army, without uniform and bearing only an armband, could venture on to the battlefield without compromising military discipline, and make themselves useful by collecting the wounded and providing first aid. This supposed dream has been realized and has passed from the realm of imagination into that of history."

Louis Appia, a member of the Committee of Five

Recognized the world over is the symbol of the Red Cross, shown below as part of a badge of the International Committee of the Red Cross. The first idea for the emblem was a white armband worn on the left arm. This was rejected beause it might cause confusion with the white flag of truce.

17

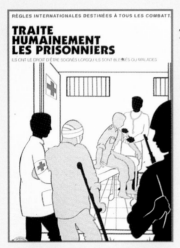

Impartiality ▶

The movement does not discriminate among race, nationalities, religious beliefs, class, or political opinions. It is guided solely by the needs of suffering people and gives priority to those most urgently in need.

▲ Humanity

The International Red Cross and Red Crescent Movement aims to prevent and alleviate human suffering wherever it may be found. It protects life and health and ensures respect for all humans. It promotes mutual understanding, friendship, cooperation, and peace among all peoples.

Neutrality ▶

In order to enjoy the confidence of all, the movement does not take sides in hostilities and does not take part in political, racial, religious, or ideological disputes. The Red Cross flags decorating the front of this Islamic hospital in Tripoli proclaim its neutrality during the shelling of Lebanon in April 1986.

Germany, the Red Cross provides, through both paid workers and volunteers, a large part of the emergency rescue services from road accident cover to mountain rescue.

The seven rules

As an international movement, the Red Cross and Red Crescent has to operate and be accepted in countries with vastly different political beliefs and systems, different religions, different customs, and different cultures. To incorporate these it is held together by seven principles that underlie all its work: *humanity, impartiality, neutrality, independence, voluntary service, unity,* and *universality.*

◀ Voluntary Service
The movement is a voluntary relief movement. Volunteers from National Societies respond to the needs of people in their own communities.

Unity ▶
There can be only one Red Cross or Red Crescent Society in each country. Here, Lebanese Red Cross volunteers provide help regardless of any warring factions.

◀ Independence
National Societies are subject to the laws of their countries but maintain their independence so that they can act according to the principles of the movement.

▲ Universality
The movement, in which all societies have equal status and share equal responsibilities and duties in helping one another, is worldwide.

However, it was all very well to draw up, in peacetime, an international agreement and for a number of countries to sign it, but how well would the agreement hold in wartime? It did not take long to find out.

In 1870, war broke out between two major European powers: Prussia and France. It was a struggle between the two countries for control of western Europe. Both countries had a National Red Cross Society, and both had signed the Geneva Convention. But their readiness for war differed sharply. The Prussian Red Cross, like the Prussian army, was well equipped and well organized. The French Red Cross, like the French army, was unprepared and badly equipped, and frantically tried to pull itself together when war broke out. But it had

The Battle of Sedan on September 1, 1870, was the decisive confrontation of the Franco-Prussian War. It ended with the surrender of the French army and of Emperor Napoleon III himself. Of the twenty-six thousand soldiers killed or wounded, about two-thirds were French. This print shows Belgian Red Cross volunteers at a casualty clearing station.

too few volunteers who had received training, and was forced to accept almost anyone who came forward. The supplies needed by these teams failed to reach them, and the whole system quickly broke down. On the battlefield, the French army had failed to equip its own medical teams with Red Cross emblems for themselves and their vehicles. In addition, it had not explained the meaning of the Red Cross worn by medical staff and volunteers from the Prussian side.

The Prussians, by contrast, had equipped all their military medical teams with Red Cross emblems and had issued instructions to its soldiers to respect French Red Cross teams and wounded French troops.

According to the official history of the ICRC, there were many violations of the 1864 Geneva Convention on both sides, but particularly by the French. As the Prussians advanced across France, there were stories of Red Cross armbands being distributed freely to French people, almost as if they were lucky charms that would protect them from the enemy. One French general, surrounded by Prussian troops, disguised himself as a Red Cross medical volunteer to make his escape. A French Red Cross organizer was attacked by his own people, who suspected that he was using his Red Cross emblem as a cover for spying, and horrifying tales were told of men wearing Red Cross armbands going on to the battlefield to kill and rob the wounded.

It was not surprising that when the Franco-Prussian War was over questions were asked about how much the Geneva Convention was worth. It had not prevented hideous suffering, and the Red Cross emblem had been widely abused or ignored.

The efforts of the National Societies of countries not directly involved in the war, however, showed the International Red Cross Movement in a better light. They raised funds for supplies and medical teams to be sent to the wounded on both sides, sometimes sending fully equipped medical units staffed with surgeons, doctors, and nurses.

In Basel, Switzerland, the ICRC embarked on a new aspect of its work. Back in 1859, Jean-Henri Dunant had been concerned that there was no system to let the families of soldiers who had been killed, wounded, or taken prisoner know what had happened. During the Franco-Prussian War, the Basel office of the Red Cross obtained and exchanged lists of prisoners from each side and passed them to the other so that families could be informed. It also set up a system for forwarding letters to and from prisoners' families at home.

The end of the Red Cross?

But it was the abuses of the Geneva Convention and the misuse of the Red Cross emblem that came to the fore when the performance of the movement in its first real test was examined. Some of the earlier critics said that the war had proved that making rules for war simply did not work. The experiment had been a failure, they said, and the sooner the Geneva Convention was allowed to fade away, the better.

The armband approved by the diplomatic conference in 1864 was first used in the war between Prussia and Denmark two years later. It was worn by Dr. Louis Appia, a member of the original Committee of Five. This war also saw the first use of a new kind of ambulance fitted with wheeled stretchers that could be taken onto the battlefield to collect the wounded.

The capture of Jerusalem by Christian soldiers in 1099 during the First Crusade. The last hours of the battle were particularly vicious, and it was said that the blood of the conquered ran down the streets, splashing the victors as they rode through it. It was no wonder that the red cross emblem of the Christians became a hated symbol in the Islamic world and could not be accepted as standing for humanity and peace.

Inside the International Red Cross Movement, too, there was disappointment. To some, it seemed that the simple aim that had inspired its founder, Jean-Henri Dunant — to relieve the suffering of soldiers wounded in battle — had been proved unworkable in practice, and they lost heart. Some supporters of the movement drifted away to form new organizations aimed at preventing war altogether. Others took up other kinds of charitable work that they felt were more rewarding.

In a way, the movement had become a victim of its own high hopes. Later, in the wars of the twentieth century, the world would learn that although the movement is not always able to persuade warring nations to observe the Geneva Conventions, and although the Red Cross emblem is occasionally misused, the fate of people caught up in war is very much better than if the Red Cross/Red Crescent did not exist.

Meanwhile, after the Franco-Prussian War, the ICRC in Geneva began the task of painstakingly rebuilding the confidence of ordinary people and their governments in the Red Cross Movement and its principles. And steadily, in the years after the war, the movement began to expand again.

The Red Crescent

When the states participating in the diplomatic conference of 1864 adopted the red cross as a uniform symbol to protect military ambulances and medical personnel in time of war, they had not intended it to have any religious meaning. They had simply adapted it from the Swiss national flag as a tribute to the home of the movement, and had not given it any Christian significance. It was a simple design that crossed language frontiers and instantly conveyed its meaning to everybody. It could be easily made from cloth for flags or painted on tents, buildings, or vehicles.

In the early years of the Geneva Conventions, the symbol presented no problem, as the first signatories were all Christian countries. If anyone saw any Christian meaning in the red cross it did not matter, because the aims of the movement were in line with the ideals of Christianity. However, in some countries the cross had a deeper and more sinister historical significance. It had been the symbol of the great Crusades conducted by Christianity against Islam between 1096 and 1291. To the people of several Islamic countries, a cross was a threat, and those who wore one were seen as enemies.

In 1876, war broke out between Turkey and Montenegro, Serbia, and Romania. Turkey had organized a National Red Cross Society in 1868, but until war broke out it had no activities. The Montenegrans, Serbs, and Romanians quickly formed National Societies of their own to carry out humanitarian work at the front. But, at first, the results were disastrous. Remembering their history, Turkish troops attacked the teams carrying Red Cross flags. "Far from serving as a protection against the destructive fury which seems to impel the Turks," the Serbian foreign minister reported, "the Red Cross flag particularly inflames their anger." There were reports of Turkish soldiers

Above: The International Federation of the Red Cross and Red Crescent emblem

Below: The Red Crescent flies over a camp for Bulgarian Muslim families who fled into Turkey. More than three hundred thousand refugees were given first aid by the Turkish Red Crescent Society.

killing Red Cross volunteers and then removing their armbands and slashing the red cross to pieces.

In a subsequent official statement, Turkey announced that, while respecting the red cross sign protecting enemy ambulances, it would use the red crescent on a white background for its own ambulances. At the same time, an Ottoman Society for Relief to Military Wounded and Sick was founded in Constantinople. It adopted the red crescent.

A diplomatic conference, which convened in 1929 to revise the Geneva Conventions, gave its sanction to this situation and also accepted the emblem and distinctive sign for the medical service of armed forces. Later the name of the movement was officially changed to the International Red Cross and Red Crescent Movement.

The United States joins in

In 1881, the International Red Cross Movement took a momentous step into a country outside Europe. It was largely due to an American woman whose experience of war had been similar to Jean-Henri Dunant's. Clara Barton was working in the United

States federal government office in Washington, D.C., when the Civil War broke out in 1861. Shocked by stories reaching Washington of the shortage of medical supplies on the battlefield, she organized the funding and movement of medical aid to the front for the rest of the war. At considerable risk to her own life, she made innumerable trips to the various battlefields in order to provide assistance to the wounded. When the Civil War ended in 1865, she set up an office to record where dead soldiers had been buried and to trace the whereabouts of those who had not returned home.

It was on a visit to Europe in 1869 that Clara Barton first heard of the Red Cross. North America, in those days, was quite isolated from the rest of the world and European ideas did not spread easily across the Atlantic. But as an international organization dedicated to the work she had tried to do on her own in America, the Red Cross captured Clara Barton's imagination. When the Franco-Prussian War broke out in 1870 she offered her help. Her offer was received less enthusiastically than she had hoped, so with a Swiss nurse she went out into the battlefields to find out for herself where she

Above: Bloody hand-to-hand fighting was foremost in the Civil War

25

could be of service. Challenged by a French sentry, she made her own makeshift Red Cross armband out of a red ribbon that she happened to be wearing, in the fashion of the time, around her throat.

While women were welcomed as Red Cross nurses behind the lines, they were regarded as a nuisance on the battlefield itself, and many times Clara was turned back. But Clara Barton was a forceful character who wouldn't take no for an answer, and by the sheer force of her personality she overcame all objections. She spent nearly four years in France and Germany, organizing hospitals and relief work and staying on after the Franco-Prussian War was over, so that she could help with the welfare of the war-ravaged cities.

She returned to the United States in 1873 determined to set up a National Red Cross Society there. It took her eight years. An American observer had attended the 1863 conference in Geneva, but

Above: Another symbol used during battle, the white flag is held up as a sign for surrender during a skirmish in the war.

the United States had not signed the Geneva Convention. Many people in America thought of the Red Cross as a European organization — and the United States had been founded and settled by people who had wanted to escape from Europe. Some military commanders made the same objections to the presence of Red Cross teams on the battlefield that had already been heard in Europe. Others quoted the "failures" of the Geneva Convention in the Franco-Prussian War.

At last, in 1881 the American Association of the Red Cross was founded with Clara Barton as its first president, and the following year the United States government signed the Geneva Convention.

The problems of peace

Then, there was a development that was to alter the whole history of the international movement. Jean-Henri Dunant's initial concern had been for the wounded on the battlefield. In a fast-growing number of countries, National Societies were training volunteers ready to move into action to treat wounded troops. Clara Barton joined others who asked: Why let this training go to waste in times of peace? In Europe, she had seen that the need for welfare work continued when the fighting was over. There were many occasions, such as accidents and natural disasters, when the skills of trained volunteers would be valuable. And there were many Red Cross and Red Crescent Societies at work in countries that would never be the scene of battles.

The idea had been considered before, but the ICRC had turned it down as early as 1865. The committee feared that if National Societies concerned themselves with peacetime disasters, their ability to deal with wartime conditions might be harmed. It suggested that other volunteer groups should be formed for peacetime purposes.

Clara Barton thought otherwise. The needs of the civilian victims of natural disasters were basically the same as those of wounded troops, she argued. The skills of trained volunteers and the medical and relief supplies available through the

Opposite: The Franco-Prussian War in 1870. Red Cross workers bring wounded soldiers back to Paris after a battle outside the city. Many countries sent teams of Red Cross volunteers to the war front, including Switzerland, Russia, Luxembourg, Ireland, and the Netherlands.

The Nobel Peace Prize, awarded for "activities of the greatest benefit to humanity," has been received four times: The first Nobel Peace Prize was awarded in 1901 to Jean-Henri Dunant and Frédéric Passy. The ICRC received the prize in 1917 and 1944 in recognition of its activities during World War I and World War II. In 1963, in the movement's centennial year, the prize was awarded jointly to the ICRC and the League of Red Cross Societies (now the International Federation).

27

Above: First aid for Japanese casualties during the Russo-Japanese War of 1904-1905.
Below: The Red Cross helping the wounded in Morocco in 1907

National Societies should be used to relieve suffering in both peace and war. The question was not whether suffering people were the victims of war or peace; it was whether their suffering could be lessened by volunteer action. Clara Barton put her ideas to the 1884 international conference in Geneva. From then on National Societies took on the duties that they carry out today.

Clara Barton was soon at work putting the wider role of the Red Cross and Red Crescent into practice. In 1887, in response to an outbreak of deadly yellow fever in Florida, she set up emergency hospitals and health services there. Two years later, the American Red Cross brought relief to the victims of the disastrous Johnstown flood in Pennsylvania, and in 1891 provided assistance to the victims of a famine in Russia. Within thirty years, Jean-Henri Dunant's plan to help the wounded in wartime was giving aid in peacetime as well.

The spread of war

The main concern of the ICRC continued to be connected with war. Europe was in turmoil as nations struggled for independence and ethnic groups claimed the right to govern themselves. Meanwhile, industrialization created demands for new sources of raw materials and new markets. The old European empires were breaking up in bloodshed. As the nineteenth century ended, war spread farther afield: The British fought the Boers in South Africa, the Spanish and Americans fought over Cuba, the Japanese attacked the Chinese province of Korea, and in 1904, war broke out between Japan and Russia.

However, the discoveries of the French chemist, Louis Pasteur, and of Joseph Lister in Great Britain regarding the importance of sterilizing wounds, brought about a revolution in the treatment of war-wounded. The development of painkillers made surgery a more demanding profession. The willing amateurs on whom the Red Cross had relied in the past needed to be supplemented by professional workers, and in many countries the Red Cross and

Red Crescent Societies set up teaching hospitals to train people.

The nature of war was also changing with the development of new weapons. The second half of the nineteenth century saw great "improvements" in the performance, accuracy, and speed of fire of the rifle. In 1889, the first fully automatic machine gun was invented, firing over six hundred rounds a minute. Heavier field guns, bringing greater death and injury to the battlefield, were developed, with more destructive kinds of explosive shells. These developments greatly increased the number of soldiers likely to be wounded on the battlefield, and this, in turn, changed the needs of battlefield medical teams. More facilities were needed to transport wounded soldiers to hospitals behind the lines, and more beds were needed in the hospitals.

At sea, the leading nations had taken advantage of steam power to reequip their navies with ever larger, ever more heavily protected warships. These new warships were less vulnerable to enemy fire, but if their protection was pierced the ships sank

The last and greatest battle of the Russo-Japanese War was fought at Mukden in Manchuria, where the Russian forces were severely mauled. There were some 97,000 Russian casualties compared with about half that number of Japanese. Here, Red Cross workers inspect the lines of Russian dead after the battle.

29

World War I brought casualties in horrific numbers. Protected by their Red Cross armbands, the nursing staff in France, above; below, ambulance men in "no man's land" between the opposing front lines.

more quickly. The Geneva Convention of 1864 had already been extended with a second Geneva Convention in 1899, to cover sailors wounded or shipwrecked at sea in wartime. But the International Committee now also wanted to have hospital ships, protected by large red crosses or crescents painted on the hull and superstructure, close to naval battle zones.

Then, in November 1911, came an ominous new development. Italy was at war with Turkey in the North African province of Tripolitania. The Turkish Red Crescent had set up military hospitals in the region, clearly marked with the Red Crescent symbol. On November 22, it was reported that Italian aircraft had bombed these hospitals. It was the first use of aircraft in war, and clearly showed that new Geneva Convention rules were needed to cover aerial warfare.

The world at war

These new rules had not been laid down, however, before World War I broke out in August 1914. After the initial excitement of the early battles and the hope of a quick peace settlement, it became clear that Europe had entered into a major war. It would probably last several years and would cover not only the whole continent of Europe, but also areas beyond, such as Africa, where the great European colonial powers were locked in rivalry.

Of sixty-five million people who fought in the war worldwide, eight and a half million were killed and another twenty-nine million were wounded, imprisoned, or missing. World War I also brought to the battlefield new weapons of war, such as the tank, introduced by the British army in 1916 and rapidly copied by other warring nations, and — most horrifying of all — poison gas. At sea, submarines were used in warfare for the first time, and aircraft — including Germany's zeppelin airships — were used to bomb civilian and military targets.

This was "total war" — a whole new kind of warfare. Previously, the pattern had been a series of separate battles. If neither side was defeated,

the armies would withdraw to reorganize and rearm before fighting again. In World War I, this pattern changed. In western and eastern Europe, the armies of the warring nations faced each other for year after year, struggling to gain or regain a piece of ground. Recklessly, each side poured more men and weapons into the long-drawn-out battle. Casualties — dead, wounded, and prisoners — were numbered in hundreds of thousands in the space of days, and by the end of 1916 there were over seven million on the western front alone. In one week in 1916, the Russian army, fighting on the eastern European front, took two hundred thousand Austro-Hungarian prisoners. The same year saw the Battle of the Somme in northern France, in which there were sixty thousand British casualties on the very first day. These figures represented human suffering on a scale that had never been experienced before. The war was the greatest challenge to the Red Cross and Red Crescent so far, and the hardest test yet for the power of the Geneva Convention to alleviate the suffering

The United States joined in the fighting of World War I in 1917 on the British and French side, but from the start it sent volunteers and equipment to the front. The war was only a few days old when the American Red Cross offered to send doctors and nurses with hospital units to help the National Societies of the countries involved.

The flamethrower was among the deadly new weapons introduced during World War I. It was first used by German troops and later adopted by the French and British. As weapons, flamethrowers were not very efficient, but they inspired fear and caused terrible burn injuries among opposing troops.

caused by armed conflict.

The number of casualties soon proved beyond the ability of the military medical units to cope with, and the National Societies of the nations at war tried to fill the gap with their own supplies, personnel, hospitals, and ambulances. The societies of neutral nations such as Sweden, Norway, Switzerland, and Spain — with the United States until it entered the war in 1917 — sent supplies and other aid to both sides. But contributions were not enough to prevent huge suffering and much needless loss of life. The ability of the "civilized" world to wage war had far outstripped that of the International Red Cross and Red Crescent Movement to ease the pain.

But there was a brighter side: It was reported that the Red Cross and Red Crescent symbols were respected on the battlefields, and medical teams were allowed to carry on with their work without interference.

Missing persons

One of the first actions of the ICRC at the outbreak of war was to reopen its office to trace dead, wounded, and missing soldiers and to report any news to their families. Run by over one thousand volunteer workers, it collected information on casualties and tried to match this up with the thousands of inquiries about missing relatives. In time, the missing persons came to include not only members of the armed forces, but also civilians who had become trapped in the fighting or behind enemy lines.

This tracing service was a mammoth task in the precomputer age, depending on millions of cards in index files that all had to be sorted and matched by hand. By the end of the war, the number of cards had reached seven million. Some cards gave complete and detailed information on individual casualties, or on people whose whereabouts were being sought. On other cards, the information was sketchy, sometimes inaccurate, or confused because of language differences or similar names.

The example of one common French surname, Martin, illustrates the difficulty faced by the tracing agency. Volunteers dealing with French casualties filled in over eight thousand cards for soldiers with the last name of Martin — and eight hundred of these were for men named Jean Martin! The only solution to a problem like this was a painstaking search of casualty lists regiment by regiment, although even this was not always successful. At one stage, it was discovered that among French prisoners of war in a single German camp there were forty prisoners named Martin, several from the same regiment, of whom fifteen had the same first name.

The Belgian section of the International Prisoner of War Agency in Geneva during World War I. The Agency oversaw the forwarding of letters, parcels, and money to both military and civilian prisoners of war, organized the return of badly wounded prisoners to their own countries, and dealt with inquiries from relatives of missing personnel.

François's story

Just how painstaking the work of tracing prisoners could be is illustrated by the story of just one French soldier, Corporal François Tessare. He was just twenty-two when he was reported missing a few weeks after war broke out in 1914. His girlfriend, Luçette Bonton, happened to be living in Geneva,

The long, drawn-out Battle of Verdun between the French and German armies lasted from February to December 1916. The opposing forces blasted away at each other, sometimes gaining a little ground and sometimes losing it. Both sides threw more and more soldiers into the battle. In the end, Verdun was saved for France, but at a huge cost in casualties on both sides. These German prisoners of war were just a few of the many thousands.

and when she had heard nothing from François for two months she went to the Red Cross Prisoner of War Agency for help.

Luçette's first visit was a disappointment. There was no trace of Corporal Tessare among the index cards that listed French casualties and prisoners of war. But the agency volunteer took down François's details and promised to make inquiries. Among the things that Luçette shyly confessed to him was that François had a nickname, Zigzag.

A week later, Luçette was back again, asking if there was any news. Again, she was disappointed. François's name had not yet appeared on any list. The agency volunteer promised that he would let her know if it did, but meanwhile she was welcome to call in if this made the wait for news easier for her.

Every Wednesday without fail, Luçette turned up at the agency to be told that there was nothing further to report. Then, after six weeks, came a blow: A thorough check had been made, and there was no Corporal François Tessare being held in any German prisoner-of-war camp or military hospital. Nor was his name on the list of soldiers who had been buried on the battlefield.

Luçette continued to call in once a week, just in case. The weeks went by. Then, one day, there was a breakthrough. One of the ways that the agency traced prisoners was to note the name of any comrades mentioned in the prisoners' letters that passed through its hands. These names were then added to the lists of known casualties, in the hope that more information would eventually turn up. One of the agency workers had spotted the mention of a French prisoner named Zigzag in a letter from another prisoner in a camp near Brussels. This man, the letter said, had suffered a severe head wound, and although he had recovered he was unable to remember who he was. The only name he could remember was Zigzag.

The agency volunteer wrote at once to the commandant of the Brussels camp, giving full details of François Tessare and asking for help in finding out whether François and Zigzag were the same man. More weeks went by. At her Wednesday meetings, Luçette fought back tears of disappointment when told that there was, as yet, no reply. Then, three months after her first call at the office, there was good news. The Brussels Zigzag was indeed François, who had now recovered his memory and was in good health.

Three months later, François Tessare was one of a group of prisoners of war who were being sent home because they were no longer fit for army service. That summer, he and Luçette were married in Paris.

Prisoners of war

The ICRC was also concerned with the way prisoners of war were treated and the conditions under which they were held. It organized the sending of over two million food parcels to prisoners, inspected prisoner-of-war camps to check that conditions were tolerable, and arranged the exchange of four hundred and fifty thousand sick and wounded prisoners. The committee also had the task of checking that the Geneva Convention rules were being observed by both sides, and of investigating

The work of nurses during World War I was a more pleasant topic for popular paintings than scenes of carnage in the trenches. Behind the battle lines, however, peaceful scenes like this were rare. More often, nurses were rushed off their feet with more casualties pouring into the hospitals every hour.

any complaints about breaches. The committee reported that, generally, all the warring nations observed the convention and respected the sign of the Red Cross on the battlefield, although, as in the Franco-Prussian War, there were some abuses.

At sea, however, the picture was grimmer. Despite protests, clearly marked hospital ships from many countries were shelled, mined, or torpedoed, sometimes with heavy loss of life. The warring nations accused one another of using ships showing the red cross to transport troops or military supplies, and these accusations and counteraccusations were still raging when the war ended.

Civilians at war

The huge scale of World War I also produced a completely unexpected problem. In earlier wars, civilians had been caught up in the fighting as armies moved across their homelands, but the armies moved slowly and it was possible for many civilians to get away before battles began. In World War I,

the situation was different. The development of rail networks and the ability to move large numbers of troops quickly, and the increasing use of motorized transportation, speeded up the whole process of war. Large areas could be occupied by troops very quickly. Within a month of the outbreak of the war in 1914, German soldiers had occupied Belgium, Luxembourg, and part of northern France. Several million civilians were cut off in this occupied territory, unable to communicate with the outside world.

This was not all. The war had broken out suddenly, trapping civilians inside enemy countries. And when naval ships started attacking merchant shipping, more civilians became victims of war. Later, civilians were killed and injured in bombing raids or by shelling from enemy lines.

The plight of civilians placed the Red Cross in a difficult position. The Geneva Convention applied only to soldiers and sailors — there was no international law on the treatment of civilians. All the ICRC could do was to appeal to countries that had occupied others to treat the civilian population as prisoners of war, while doing its best to help communications between the occupied countries and outside. The ICRC could only protest in vain about the sinking of merchant ships and bombing raids on civilian targets. For the moment, modern warfare seemed to have outstripped the ability of the Geneva Convention to control it.

But hundreds of thousands of troops wounded in battle or taken prisoner, and their families at home, had good reason to be thankful that the ICRC, through the many different aspects of its work, from providing battlefield canteens to supervising conditions in prison camps, was able to bring relief to the war's victims.

Winning the peace

Wars do not end as easily and quickly as they start. The end of World War I left Europe and many other parts of the world in a state of shock. Epidemics of influenza, cholera, and typhus — made worse by the war-ravaged peoples' inability to resist infection

Above and left: Revolution in Russia in 1917 was followed by civil war and a famine that lasted from 1921 to 1923. One and a half million people fled the country, but this exodus was not enough to solve the food shortage for those left behind. In 1921, Russian farming output was only about two-thirds of what it had been in 1913. The Russian famine set the Red Cross and Red Crescent Movement firmly on the path of commitment to relieving suffering as a result of civil war as well as in wars between nations. For an organization founded to foster humanitarian aid, the dreadful reports and photographs like these that were coming out of Russia simply could not be ignored.

— raged across Europe for some years, killing more people than had died in the war. Revolution in Russia in 1917 had been followed by civil war, creating a flood of one and a half million refugees who fled across the border to nearby countries. In central and eastern Europe there was famine. In western Europe, good farming land had been made useless, churned into seas of mud by the ebb and flow of battle. Soldiers returning from the war found that there was no work for them and often that their homes had been damaged or destroyed.

An ICRC report written in 1918 outlined some of the problems to be faced in the postwar world. "In all the countries at war," it said, "there are hundreds of thousands of disabled, limbless and chronically sick persons who have to be found some means of earning a living, some forms of employment which are not beyond their greatly diminished abilities. In addition, there is a battle to be fought against the ravages of tuberculosis which daily threatens to increase the number of its victims, especially among ex-prisoners suffering from lack of food. Finally, there are all the widows and orphans, all the elderly parents, who have lost the breadwinner on whom they depended; they all need help urgently."

Although the ICRC has international responsibilities, it is a private and independent Swiss organization. All twenty-five members of the International Committee itself are Swiss citizens. The ICRC employs a staff of six hundred in Geneva and a similar number of delegates in various parts of the world, together with 2,300 employees recruited locally.

There was now no doubt that the International Red Cross and Red Crescent Movement saw it as its duty to continue its welfare work in peacetime. At the time, it was the only international organization of its kind able to coordinate the massive effort needed. Yet, even within the movement, there was a gap in the organization between the ICRC, based in Switzerland, and the National Societies in individual countries. The problems of rebuilding European economies and societies after the ravages of war demanded a greater effort than could be organized by the ICRC alone. The result was the setting-up in 1919 of what is now the third arm of the whole International Red Cross and Red Crescent Movement — the League of National Red Cross and Red Crescent Societies. In 1991 this was given the new title of the International Federation of the Red Cross and Red Crescent Societies.

Helping hands

The International Federation was initially founded at the suggestion of the chairman of the War Council of the American Red Cross, Henry P. Davison. His idea was that the National Societies in each country could learn from one another and encourage one another in their activities, not only in organizing immediate relief, but also in laying down new foundations for health care. The setting up of the International Federation sparked off new efforts, particularly in such fields as health education, child care, disease prevention, and youth activities. This was another important step forward in the development of the International Red Cross and Red Crescent Movement.

The federation added to its policy of merely reacting to the disasters of war and peace that of working to avoid human suffering and to prevent suffering as well as alleviating it. Today, over one hundred and fifty National Societies are members

The ICRC building in Geneva. ICRC stands for the International Committee of the Red Cross. The banner here is in French and shows CICR, which stands for Comité International de la Croix Rouge.

41

*The Red Cross and Red
Crescent Youth teaches
its youngest members the
symbol of humanitarian
aid, the power of group
activities, and the fun of
being part of
the organization.*

of the International Federation.

The federation was intended to echo in practical work the efforts of the League of Nations, which had also been formed after World War I. Its aim was to prevent further wars by the diplomatic settlement of disputes and the encouragement of international cooperation. In fact, this first attempt at an international peacekeeping organization was unsuccessful, and it was replaced in 1945 by the United Nations Organization. But the International Federation of Red Cross and Red Crescent Societies flourished.

It had been in existence only four years when it faced its first major test, the disastrous 1923 earthquake in Japan. The quake, and the fires that followed, killed two hundred thousand people, made millions homeless, and destroyed almost half of the city of Tokyo. This disaster set the pattern for the International Federation's work in such emergencies, acting as the link between the National Society of the afflicted country and other societies that were able to offer help.

Young people join in

From the earliest days of the International Red Cross and Red Crescent Movement, young people have been among the most willing volunteers. After the Battle of Solferino in 1859, the children of Castiglione had willingly run errands and fetched and carried supplies. In 1885, children in Bulgaria had made bandages out of old linen. Again in World War I, many children and young people had helped with Red Cross activities. In four countries (Canada, Australia, Italy, and the United States) youth sections were already specially organized. Now, it was time to find an official place for children in the movement.

Today, we are used to the idea that young people should take part in different types of community activity, but in the early years of this century it was a novel concept. In those days, the worlds of childhood and adulthood were regarded as separate. Children and teenagers belonged in the world of

school and play and were not taken seriously.

The Red Cross Movement saw things differently, and when the International Federation of Red Cross and Red Crescent Societies was founded, one of its first actions was to encourage the formation by National Societies of junior and youth sections.

This decision had three good effects that have helped to shape the International Red Cross and Red Crescent Movement as it exists today.

First, it provided a way of attracting and training enthusiastic young volunteers. Second, it made young people in particular, and society in general, more aware of the humanitarian aims and principles of the movement. Finally, it provided a channel through which young people could show their concern, in practical ways, for the welfare of others.

There are now opportunities in almost every country in the world for young people from the age of eight or nine to be actively involved members in the Red Cross/Red Crescent work. Local junior and

Training for emergency situations is an important part of Red Cross and Red Crescent Youth work. As well as training the volunteers of the future, it plays an important part in making young people aware of the movement and the principles it stands for.

During the Spanish civil war assistance was provided for both military and civilians. It was a particularly difficult situation because many countries had a policy of not intervening in Spain and also because the third Geneva Convention had not addressed the issue of civilians in wartime and internal conflicts.
However, help was given. Here relief supplies from the Swiss Red Cross arrive at Corbera de Llobregat in the mountains.

youth members can receive training in such skills as first aid and basic health care. They can also attend leadership conferences and are able to take part in all kinds of community activities and international friendship events.

Making new rules

After World War I, the International Red Cross and Red Crescent Movement had to rethink its future in many different ways. Jean-Henri Dunant's original aim of providing help to the wounded on the battlefield had expanded into action in many other areas of wartime life, and the aftermath of the war had raised new problems. For example, was it right for the ICRC to expand its activities to include civil war and internal unrest, such as took place in Russia following the 1917 revolution? The ICRC had established its right to protect and visit prisoners of war — but what about political prisoners, arrested not because they had committed any crime but because of their political beliefs, or people imprisoned, as in Germany in the 1930s, simply because of their race? World War I had introduced,

for the first time, large-scale aerial warfare. What new measures must the movement consider to cope with this development?

In 1929, a diplomatic conference was held in Geneva to update the policies of the Geneva Convention. This third Geneva Convention made it legal for aircraft being used to evacuate war wounded to be given Red Cross or Red Crescent markings. A new set of rules was laid down for the treatment of prisoners of war, including their food, clothing, medical care, the work they were allowed to do while in captivity, and their right to send and receive letters. The movement was trying to keep pace with developments in warfare — but warfare itself, and the ruthlessness with which it was carried out, was racing ahead.

Another world war

Just how true this was was soon to be revealed. Hopes that World War I would,be the "war to end all wars" were quickly dashed. In 1939 war broke out again in Europe and quickly spread to Africa, the Middle East, and Southeast Asia.

In World War I, aerial warfare had taken place on or near the battlefields. There had been some aerial attacks on civilian targets, but, in general, civilians had been accidentally caught in the cross fire. In modern warfare civilians, too, became targets. The aim of a nation at war had become not merely to defeat the armed forces of the enemy but to strike at the homes and lives of everyone in the enemy country. "The enemy" was now not only troops in trenches on the opposing lines, sailors in enemy ships, or air crews in enemy aircraft, but — for example — babies and elderly people sheltering under the stairs of their homes or families caught by bombers while out shopping. The terror produced by attacks on cities from the air had itself become a weapon of war. The development of aircraft and bombs between the wars enabled bombers to obliterate whole cities in a few hours of intensive bombing. "Total war" had taken on a new and terrible meaning.

Aerial warfare was in its infancy in World War I and was basically limited to military targets. However, by World War II, there was no pretense that raids were not being made on civilian targets as well. This "bread-basket" bomb released shells over a large area and aimed to damage as much as possible. The idea was to sap morale and the will to fight by attacking civilians in their homes, spreading fear and disrupting everyday life.

The Japanese city of Hiroshima after the first atomic bomb was dropped by an air force plane on August 6, 1945. The official history of the ICRC says: "The suddenness of the attack, the impossibility of any protection against its effects and the number of victims marked a new level in the mounting sequence of methods of destruction. Of Hiroshima nothing was left but calcined ruins...."

In Europe, invasion by German troops, led by Adolf Hitler, was preceded by merciless bombing raids on the cities and attacks from the air on refugees fleeing from the invaders. Britain and Germany set out on a campaign of bombing each other's cities regardless of the certainty of the high civilian casualties that would result. The ICRC protested against this extension of war to include innocent victims. But it had to admit that its efforts to spare civilians from the horrors of war had failed. Then, on August 6, 1945, came the most sinister news of all.

Flying high over the Japanese city of Hiroshima, an American aircraft dropped the first atomic bomb, with many times more destructive power than any raid involving hundreds of aircraft. Nothing was left of Hiroshima but charred ruins. The shock wave of the explosion, and the heat and fires that followed, killed one hundred thousand people. Tens of thousands of injured with severe burns lay

Above: In 1942, German troops reached Stalingrad, deep inside Russia. For two months the city held out, and finally the Germans retreated. But meanwhile, as this old photograph shows, every building had been destroyed and the inhabitants carried on as best they could among the ruins.

Left: When the Russians swept through eastern Germany in 1945, thousands of Germans fled to the west. This original photograph shows the refugee problem as one of the ICRC's greatest challenges after the war had ended.

Wives and mothers, photographed in 1945, display photographs and descriptions of their missing soldier husbands and sons in Friedland, Germany. The work of the ICRC's Central Tracing Agency to reunite families or at least give them some news about their loved ones went on for many years after the end of World War II.

among the ruins. Three days later, a second atomic bomb fell on the city of Nagasaki, with similar results.

The dropping of these two bombs led to the swift conclusion of World War II, which had already ended in Europe. But the dreadful effects of the explosions (some of which, such as long-term radiation sickness, were not yet fully understood) shocked the entire world.

Europe in ruins

As the American, British, French, and Russian armies drove back the German invaders in 1945, terrible facts were revealed about life under Nazi occupation. The liberating armies discovered death camps where six million Jews and half a million gypsies, as well as thousands of other civilian prisoners, had been systematically killed. The existence of these camps had been known, but with few exceptions, up to the last months of the war, the ICRC had been refused permission to visit them. That the ICRC had been able to do nothing to prevent the mass murders was a blow. However, the immediate task was to bring relief to the survivors of the death camps and to the millions of other people who needed urgent help.

Victims of war

In the last days of the war, and in the months following, Europe was full of wandering people. They included released prisoners from the concentration camps, released prisoners of war, families who had been uprooted from their homes in Nazi-occupied countries and sent to Germany to work, and hundreds of thousands who had been bombed out of the cities. Many of those who remained at home were living in ruins or makeshift shelters, without food or sufficient clothes or bedding. Providing immediate help for these needy millions became the first big postwar task for the ICRC.

The 1949 Convention

Meanwhile, what could be learned from the lessons of World War II? The Geneva Conventions had been very largely observed as far as military prisoners of war were concerned. The major exception was Japan, which had not signed the 1929 Convention. Many prisoners were treated brutally and thousands were starved or worked to death by the Japanese. But by far the greatest number of victims in the war had been civilians. Was it possible, the ICRC asked, to draw up a Convention that would protect them in time of war?

In 1949, a fourth Geneva Convention was signed with 429 sections — a vast extension of the ten articles of the original 1864 Convention. For the first time, it included provisions for the protection of civilians in wartime.

"As long as we don't live in a world where law and justice have definitely replaced wars, it is the responsibility of our Movement to speak up for the victims, and to strive constantly to bring them the protection and assistance which is their right."

Princess Christina of Sweden, 1990

Above: Three posters showing the correct treatment of wounded and prisoners.

The 1949 Convention, which is the main agreement under which the ICRC still operates, demanded protection for:
- Military wounded and sick, medical personnel, and chaplains;
- Wounded, sick, medical personnel, chaplains of armed forces at sea, and the shipwrecked;
- Prisoners of war;
- Civilians in enemy or occupied territory.

The nations signing the Convention agreed to:
- Care for friends and enemies alike;
- To respect the dignity, family rights, and religious views of all people and to protect women;
- To allow ICRC delegates to visit prisoner-of-war camps and civilian internment camps and to speak privately to people held there;
- To prohibit inhuman or degrading treatment, the taking of hostages, mass extermination, torture, executions without trial, deportations, and the wanton destruction of private property.

In 1977 a diplomatic conference added to these with two protocols that provide protection for victims of internal conflicts.

War without end?

World War II ended with the Japanese surrender on August 8, 1945. Although there has been no war on such a worldwide scale since, there has not been a single day when there hasn't been fighting somewhere in the world.

The work of the International Red Cross and Red Crescent Movement in lessening the suffering of both armed forces and civilians has gone on unceasingly. In 1991, the movement launched a world campaign to emphasize the cost of these unending wars in terms of human suffering. "Millions of people," Princess Christina of Sweden told the conference called to launch the campaign, "live daily under the dark clouds of war and armed conflict. They face death, imprisonment, separation from their families, and are forced to leave their homes or countries."

In World War I, 15 percent of war victims were

civilians. In World War II, the proportion rose to 65 percent. By 1991, it was 90 percent. In thirty-two major conflicts between or within nations in 1988-1989 alone, five million people — the majority of them civilians — were killed and thirty-two million were wounded, imprisoned, or made homeless.

The campaign highlighted the plight of just some of these victims. They included eleven-year-old Diya, a Lebanese girl, whose face was disfigured by shrapnel so badly that she dropped out of school. Another Lebanese child, Fadi, was ten when he innocently picked up what turned out to be an unexploded bomb. He is now blind. The Wilson family in Liberia fled from their home when armed soldiers began to murder local people. Now, they live as refugees forty to one room, taking turns to share the beds. And so the stories go on, of people living from day to day in the hope that there will be enough food and somewhere to shelter. The Red Cross and Red Crescent works closely with the United Nations High Commissioner for Refugees

Above: Since 1975, Lebanon has been devastated by civil war. In the capital, Beirut, bombing and shooting has terrorized the civilian population and caused countless casualties, often among people caught in cross fire. The cost to the first aid teams of the Lebanese Red Cross Society, too, has been heavy. Since 1975, eleven volunteers have been killed, eighty wounded, and six permanently disabled out of a volunteer force of 1,400. Two ICRC delegates were kidnapped and later released.

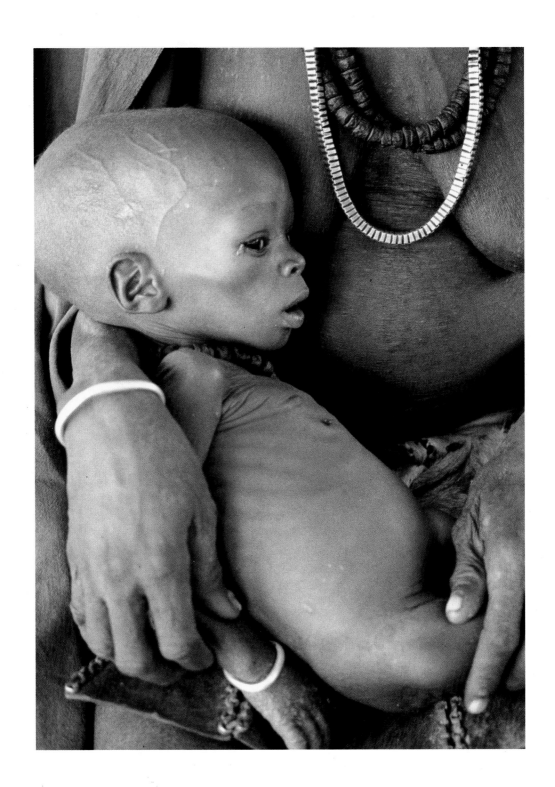

(UNHCR) not only in providing much-needed assistance, but in publicizing worldwide the appalling suffering of refugees.

Against the background of war and internal strife and the suffering they bring, and in spite of it, the International Red Cross and Red Crescent Movement is a shining example of the truth that people do care for one another. A war breaks out. A typhoon strikes. Drought brings famine. And today, Red Cross and Red Crescent teams are a familiar sight as they rush to bring help to the injured, organize rescue and medical services, distribute food and other necessities of life, and provide follow-up care for victims. Meanwhile, in cities, towns, and villages across the world, volunteers provide all kinds of help in the community, from writing letters for the blind to recruiting blood donors, from helping disabled children to organizing health clinics. The International Red Cross and Red Crescent Movement is an international network of caring people.

Top left: Refugees are a worldwide problem. This camp is temporarily home for five thousand Kurds. Top right: A Red Cross ship is loaded with supplies. Bottom: A convoy brings tents, blankets, and food for refugees.

Opposite: The drought of 1984-1985 brought famine and death to thousands of Africans. Pictures of the starving were flashed all over the world, shocking viewers. Fund-raising concerts raised much needed food aid. Today, the International Red Cross and Red Crescent Movement helps Africa help itself.

Cape Verde, off the west coast of
Africa, has suffered from drought
since 1968, and large food supplies
have to be imported. The National
Society organizes food distribution
and also has a nutrition and health
care program. Above: Mules take
food to isolated villages.
Top right: Loading up for the
journey. Middle: A home visit, with
some advice for a young mother
from a Red Cross visitor.
Right: The monthly Red Cross food
distribution

For example, twenty-two-year-old Sam-Ang Poompradom is a volunteer worker for the Thai Red Cross Society. Not only does she volunteer her services, but she also has to buy her own uniform and pay her own travel expenses.

As Sam-Ang's paid job is in the evenings, she is able to give up some of her free time during the day. On Mondays, she goes to a hospital and helps outpatients to fill in their forms for medical treatment. Many patients cannot understand the forms, so Sam-Ang explains the questions to them and writes down their answers. Thursdays find her back at the hospital again, this time to help nurses look after patients in the wards. On Fridays, she does more Red Cross work, packing equipment for the Thai Red Cross vans that travel to remote country areas to give medical and dental treatment. Sometimes, Sam-Ang admits, her Red Cross work is tiring — but she adds, "It gives me a feeling of contentment and true accomplishment. I guess I'll be a Thai Red Cross volunteer as long as my energy lasts. I'm happy here, because I know that what I do is really useful."

In Zimbabwe, one of the special projects of the National Red Cross Society is to identify and help disabled people in rural communities. Groups of volunteers go out into the villages and collect information on people's various disabilities. Volunteers are then assigned to particular families to help them to learn everyday skills, and later to acquire more advanced skills that will enable them to earn a living. Several thousand people have been helped in this way since the program began in 1984.

At Solferino, Jean-Henri Dunant saw the importance of having trained helpers, and training is still the vital element in Red Cross and Red Crescent voluntary work. As well as basic first aid and health care, volunteers specialize in training for the particular needs of their communities. In California, for example, where there is a long history of earthquakes, volunteers are specially trained to teach others safety and survival techniques. After the Chernobyl disaster in 1986, when nuclear fallout and radiation spread over a vast area, the Alliance of Red

Cross and Red Crescent Societies of the USSR
organized training for its volunteers in the use of
radiation-monitoring equipment. The message is the
same as it was in Jean-Henri Dunant's day: Human
suffering can be lessened by volunteers who are
willing to help and are trained to be effective.

Crisis in Africa

The International Red Cross and Red Crescent
Movement is also concerned with the development
of underdeveloped areas of the world. This has been
reflected in some of the problems that the
International Red Cross and Red Crescent Movement
has tackled in the past few years, particularly on the
southern edge of the Sahara Desert in Africa.
During 1984 and 1986, over one million Africans in
this region, known as the Sahel, died of starvation
or the effects of malnutrition. The beginnings of

*In 1984-1985 thousands
of starving Ethiopian
refugees were treated by
the Red Cross. A huge
operation was needed to
help these people.*

the disaster were natural — droughts since the 1960s that had turned good grassland, suitable for crops and livestock, into desert. But things were made worse by a series of civil wars and disturbances across the Sahel in Ethiopia, Chad, Sudan, Angola, Uganda, and Mozambique. These upheavals damaged farming, disrupted the transport of goods, created vast numbers of refugees who fled into nearby areas, and made it difficult — and often impossible — for aid to be distributed to those who needed it.

"Water for Life" may not help all the thirsty children in Mali, but the International Red Cross and Red Crescent Movement brings relief to as many as possible.

The crisis in Africa exactly illustrated the chain of events that so concerns the International Red Cross and Red Crescent Movement. The countries of the Sahel are poor, and even without war would not have been able to organize relief for their starving peoples. One of the causes of the wars was the struggle of competing tribes for the more productive land. The increasing desertification of the Sahel was made worse by overgrazing and overfarming. In this way, a chain of problems built up until it exploded, in 1984, into large-scale starvation.

The International Red Cross and Red Crescent Movement believes that the world needs to understand more clearly how certain human activities — bad farming practices, for example — can lead to disastrous environmental consequences, and how these consequences can be prevented. In the same way as National Societies prepare their communities to provide help to accident victims by teaching accident prevention and first aid, the International Federation highlights the problems of underdevelopment and then creates developmental plans with projects such as tree planting, the provision of clean water, and basic health care.

In the same manner, the ICRC organized a meeting in 1991 to discuss the theme of "Famine and War." The meeting noted that although the 1949 Geneva Convention forbids the use of the starvation of civilians as a method of warfare, such methods were used in various parts of the world. Military restrictions were also often used to prevent the distribution of relief supplies.

Risky work

ICRC delegates in the field are required to have had a university education and to be able to speak several languages, one of which must be English. They have to be able to negotiate, analyze a situation quickly, and show practical common sense. They must also be courageous. Their work is often carried out in the middle of fighting with only the Red Cross emblem as protection.

The delegates or representatives of the ICRC and their National Society counterparts who work in areas of war or civil disturbance run great risks. Their only protection, on their vehicles and their uniforms, is the Red Cross or Red Crescent emblem. Their safety depends on both sides on the battlefield observing the Geneva Conventions. Red Cross vehicles are not bombproof, and Red Cross personnel do not wear bulletproof jackets or carry any other protection. Their presence in risk areas is based entirely on trust.

Since 1945, seventeen ICRC delegates have been killed while on duty, and many more have been wounded, attacked, or threatened. Some of the deaths and injuries have been accidental. Delegates often have to travel over roads that may have been mined, for example. But sometimes delegates have been deliberately attacked, as happened in the Philippines in 1990 when a delegate and a Filipino employee were gunned down in cold blood.

Many disputes in the world involve "unofficial" guerrilla armies, and these are the cause of many of the Red Cross and Red Crescent casualties. Most nations make sure that their armed forces understand the meaning and importance of the Red Cross and Red Crescent emblems, and often Red Cross or Red Crescent people themselves instruct troops on how they should behave when they see a red cross or red crescent on the battlefield. But guerrilla forces often do not understand the emblems or deliberately ignore them.

Volunteers in troubled areas also take risks. Late in December 1989, a few days before the Romanian government of President Ceauşescu fell, Romanian secret police were still attacking rebel forces and protesters. A forty-four-year-old Hungarian Red Cross volunteer, Sandor Toth, accidentally strayed into this fight on his way to deliver a consignment of relief supplies from the Hungarian Red Cross. He was shot dead by the secret police, one of many volunteer workers in recent years to have been killed while carrying out humanitarian work.

In recent years, Sudan has had to cope with war, famine, drought, floods, epidemics, and a plague of locusts. The ICRC, the International Federation of Red Cross and Red Crescent Societies, the Sudanese Red Crescent, and a number of individual National Societies have cooperated in a far-reaching project that includes health posts where advice on nutrition can be given and basic health checks carried out.

Taking care

One ICRC delegate who has worked in many parts of the world says that extreme care is the key to survival. "We all know the risks we run," he says. "We learn all about them in our training. But when we go into the field we're given a very detailed set of safety rules, and it's up to us to follow them as closely as possible. For example, if we're going into a dangerous area we make sure we give advance warning to anyone who may be interested, and get permission from each and every one of them. When I was working in Afghanistan, where there were any number of different small guerrilla groups, each under its own commander, I sometimes had to let fifteen groups know that I was coming before I made a move.

"You must never let yourself be lulled into a

false sense of security in this job, however tired you may be. You need to keep on the alert all the time for unusual activity or unusual quiet or just things that somehow don't add up.

"And the last key thing is: you must not hesitate to turn back if things start to go wrong or something unusual crops up. You can always check the situation from a safe distance and try again another time."

A place for everyone

The Red Cross and Red Crescent delegates and volunteers who venture into areas of war or civil conflict are the heroes and heroines of the movement. By their acts they express a concern for human beings that stretches back from the world's battlefields to almost every community in almost every country. For in every community, there are people who need help.

In the remote villages of Thailand, it may be eye treatment or dental care, advice on feeding a sick child, or looking after an elderly relative. In the cities of Germany or the United States, help may be vital for drug addicts who need to kick the habit. In Africa, where more than seven million people are HIV positive, the Red Cross and Red Crescent Societies provide much-needed support for AIDS' victims and their families.

And in countless countries across the world, Red Cross and Red Crescent adult and youth volunteers perform important though less urgent tasks: providing library services in hospitals, organizing transport to clinics for elderly or disabled patients, running day-care facilities and play schools, maintaining lending arrangements for wheelchairs and other medical equipment, and keeping their first aid and nursing training up-to-date for use in emergencies.

Worldwide, there are more than one hundred million people involved in Red Cross and Red Crescent volunteer activities, proving what Jean-Henri Dunant discovered at Solferino more than one hundred and thirty years ago: that people are willing to help if someone will show them the way.

The distribution between victims of war and those of peace has become blurred today. Food has become a weapon in many civil wars, from Africa to Yugoslavia, together with the denial of medical and other vital supplies to civilian populations. The Red Cross and Red Crescent Movement offers aid unstintingly to all who suffer, military or civilian, in peace or war.

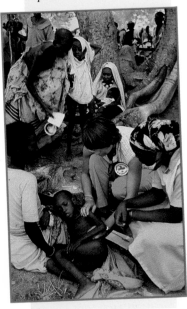

Glossary

Aftershock: A lesser shock following the main shock of an earthquake.

Chaplain: A clergyman in uniform who serves the armed forces.

Cholera: An often fatal disease caused by drinking or cooking with, contaminated water.

Concentration camp: A prison camp which, in Germany, under Adolf Hitler, housed Jews, gypsies, and other prisoners, most of whom were killed.

Convention: A formal international agreement.

Crusades: A series of "holy wars" that took place between 1096 and 1291. They were conducted by Christian European rulers against Islam over the control of the Holy Land.

Delegate: The term used by the International Red Cross and Red Crescent Movement for a representative in the field.

Desertification: The return of fertile land to a desert.

Federation: A league or union of several groups for common action.

Fundamental Principles: The code of the International Red Cross and Red Crescent Movement; they are *Humanity,* Impartiality, Neutrality, Independence, Voluntary Service, Unity, and Universality.

Geneva Conventions: International treaties which lay down rules, valid in conflict, to protect people who do not take part in the fighting (civilians) or who no longer take part (the wounded and sick, prisoners of war). The Geneva Convention of 1864 dealt with the protection of the wounded and sick on the battlefield. It was later extended to include victims of war at sea (1899) and prisoners of war (1929).

In 1949 a major revision took place, resulting in four conventions, covering the wounded and sick on land and at sea, prisoners of war, and civilians in enemy-controlled territories. In 1977 the conventions were updated and amended by two protocols to take account of modern warfare developments. Some 165 nations (out of 171) are now party to the conventions.

Guerrilla: An unofficial soldier who is not normally attached to any government and is usually involved in independent acts of harassment and sabotage.

Humanitarian: Concerned with human life and happiness.

Humanity: One of the *Fundamental Principles* of the International Red Cross and Red Crescent Movement that requires members to prevent and relieve suffering, and to promote friendship, peace, and understanding around the world.

ICRC — International Committee of the Red Cross: This developed from the Committee of Five who met in Geneva in February 1863. It is a private, all-Swiss governed, nonpolitical, independent institution. It acts as a neutral intermediary in *humanitarian* matters during international conflicts, civil wars, and internal disturbances.

IFRC — International Federation of the Red Cross and Red Crescent Societies: The IFRC promotes the *humanitarian* activities of National Societies. It organizes and coordinates international Red Cross and Red Crescent relief for victims of disasters and refugees outside areas of conflict.

National Societies: Each country in the world can have its own Red Cross or Red Crescent Society, provided certain conditions are met. These include upholding the *Fundamental Principles* of the movement and using the appropriate symbol.

Neutral: Not taking sides in wars or conflicts or getting involved in political, racial, or religious arguments.

Protocol: A diplomatic agreement between countries.

Prussia: The part of Europe that we know today as Germany was divided into thirteen large and twenty-five little states in the nineteenth century. The largest was Prussia, which was divided into two main blocks around Cologne and Berlin respectively. It was also a large area in what is now Poland. Gradually, Prussia extended its influence and, in 1870, the German Empire was founded as a confederation of all states under the king of Prussia.

Radiation sickness: Damage to the body tissues, caused by exposure to radiation, that is eventually fatal.

Signatory: A diplomat who signs a document on behalf of his or her country, or a government bound with other nation states by a signed treaty or convention.

Tuberculosis: A disease of the lungs that was often fatal before the discovery of penicillin.

Typhus: An often fatal infectious disease that is usually found among people in dirty, overcrowded conditions.

Violation: Breaking of the rules.

Yellow fever: A serious tropical disease caused by mosquito bites.

Important Dates

1828	May 8: Jean-Henri Dunant is born in Geneva, Switzerland.
1859	June 24: The Battle of Solferino. Jean-Henri Dunant is present and helps to relieve the suffering of the wounded.
1861-1865	The Civil War. Clara Barton becomes interested in welfare work for prisoners and the wounded.
1862	Jean-Henri Dunant's book, *A Memory of Solferino,* is published. In it, he puts forward ways of helping the wounded in wartime.
1863	Feb 17: The first meeting of the Committee of Five, formed to give support to Dunant's ideas, takes place in Geneva. Oct 23: An international conference, called to launch the Red Cross Movement, opens in Geneva. It is attended by representatives from sixteen countries. A red cross on a white background is adopted as the movement's symbol.
1864	Aug 22: The first Geneva Convention is signed by representatives of twelve countries.
1870-1871	The Franco-Prussian War. The Red Cross begins its work of tracing and reporting on prisoners of war. Clara Barton is active in providing relief on the battlefields.
1873	Clara Barton returns to the United States and begins her campaign to set up a Red Cross Society there.
1875	The Geneva Committee adopts the title "International Committee of the Red Cross."
1876	The red crescent is first used as an alternative emblem to the red cross in Islamic countries.
1881	The American Association of the Red Cross is founded, with Clara Barton as president.
1882	The United States signs the Geneva Convention.
1899	A conference in The Hague extends the Geneva Convention to those wounded or shipwrecked in naval warfare.
1906	The first Geneva Convention is revised at a conference in Geneva.
1907	The Hague Convention introduces legal protection for prisoners of war.
1910	Oct 30: Jean-Henri Dunant dies, in Switzerland, at age eighty-two.
1914-1918	World War I. The ICRC sets up its Prisoner of War Agency. Thousands of volunteers are mobilized to serve on the battlefields.
1917	The ICRC receives the Nobel Peace Prize.
1919	The League (now the International Federation) of Red Cross and Red Crescent National Societies is founded.
1929	A third Geneva Convention lays down rules to protect and care for prisoners of war.
1936-1939	The Spanish civil war. The International Red Cross (comprising the ICRC, the League, and National Societies) provides relief and protection activities. These are a forerunner of its World War II operations.

1939-1945	World War II. The ICRC again checks observance of the Geneva Conventions, traces and protects prisoners of war, and handles prisoners' mail. National Societies and the League organize food parcels and, at the end of the war, bring relief to millions of refugees.
1944	The ICRC wins the Nobel Peace Prize for the second time.
1948	May 8: The first celebration of the World Red Cross and Red Crescent Day (the birth date of Jean-Henri Dunant).
1949	Four Geneva Conventions are adopted, covering the wounded in land warfare, the wounded and shipwrecked at sea, prisoners of war, and civilians in enemy or occupied territory.
1960	The Prisoner of War Agency is renamed the Central Tracing Agency and becomes a permanent unit of the ICRC.
1963	At the time of the 100th anniversary of the first Geneva Convention the ICRC and the League (now the International Federation) are jointly awarded the Nobel Peace Prize.
1977	A diplomatic conference in Geneva adopts two Protocols giving further protection to civilians in time of war and to victims and participants in internal conflicts.
1986	The International Red Cross is officially renamed the "The International Red Cross and Red Crescent Movement."
1988	Earthquake strikes Armenia resulting in 25,000 deaths. International aid helps rebuild homes, schools, and hospitals.
1990-1991	Gulf War, the movement's activities include refugee relief, protection of civilians, medical assistance, prisoner of war exchanges, food and water distribution.

How you can help

If you would like to help the International Red Cross and Red Crescent Movement in its work at home or abroad, you should contact your own National Society.

Look in your local telephone directory under "Red Cross" (or "Red Crescent") and contact them to ask how you can join and help. Most areas have a Red Cross or Red Crescent Youth section where young people can learn first aid and basic lifesaving techniques. They also hold regular fund-raising events.

Your local Red Cross or Red Crescent office should also be able to give you additional information and project material.

The following books and others about the Red Cross/ Red Crescent can be ordered through the local Red Cross/ Red Crescent office:

A Memory of Solferino by Jean-Henri Dunant (Geneva: ICRC); *Warrior without Weapons* by Marcel Junod (Geneva: ICRC); *Red Cross and Red Crescent: Portrait of an International Movement* (Geneva: ICRC/Federation); *Red Cross, Red Crescent* magazine (Geneva: Federation/ICRC).

Index

American Association of the
Red Cross 27, 28, 41

Barton, Clara 24, 27, 28
and American Civil War 25
and Franco-Prussian War
25-26
and setting up of American
Red Cross 26-27

Committee of Five 13, 14

Davison, Henry P. 41
Dunant, Jean-Henri 10, 22,
28, 44, 55, 56, 60
and Battle of Solferino
10-12
and Committee of Five 13
writes *A Memory of
Solferino* 12-13

Franco-Prussian War 19-21,
22

Geneva Conventions 22, 24,
31, 35, 38, 49, 58, **61**
First (1864) 15, 19, 30, 49
criticism of 15-17
signed by United States
27
violations of 20-21, 36
Second (1899) 30
Third (1929) 24, 45
Fourth (1949) 49-50, 58

Hiroshima 46-48
Hitler, Adolf 46

League of Nations 42

A Memory of Solferino 12-13

Nagasaki 48
Napoleon III, Emperor 10

Ottoman Society for Relief to
Military Wounded and Sick
24

Red Cross, American
Association of the 27
Red Cross and Red
Crescent Movement,
International 24
accepts use of red
crescent 23-24

adopts red cross as
symbol 14-15, 22-23
birth of 9-13
dangers for delegates
58-60
development of activities
27-28, 40-42, 50
and Franco-Prussian War
19-20
Geneva Conventions
adopted by
First (1864) 15, 19, 30
violations of 20-21, 36
Second (1899) 30
Third (1929) 24, 45
Fourth (1949) 49-50, 58
international conferences
14, 15, 22, 24, 28
and Iranian earthquake
7-8
National Societies **61**
formation of 15
role of 17
setting up of youth
sections 42-44
training of volunteers
17-18, 55-56
work of 28, 55
principles of 18, **61**
provides relief for African
drought victims 55-58
role of 8-9, 53
role of children in 42-44
and UNHCR 51-52
work of 8-9, 50-58, **61**
and World War I 31-32,
36-38
and World War II 46, 48-49
Red Cross, International
Committee of the (ICRC)
17, 20, 38, 40, **61**
dangers for delegates
58-60
role of 17, 42, 44-45, 49
and welfare of prisoners
of war 21, 32-35, 44
Red Cross and Red
Crescent Societies,
International Federation
of 8, 40, 41, 43, **61**
role of 17, 58

Solferino, Battle of 9-10, 42
Jean-Henri Dunant's
reaction to 10-12

United Nations High
Commissioner for Refugees
(UNHCR) 51-52
United Nations Organization
42

World War I 30-32, 36-38, 42,
44, 45
aftermath of 38-40
casualties of 30, 31-32, 50
role of Red Cross in 31-32,
36-38
World War II 45-49
aftermath of 49
casualities of 45, 46, 51
role of Red Cross in 46,
48-49
use of atomic bombs in
46-48